THE
IRISH WRITERS'
QUOTATION BOOK

THE
IRISH WRITERS'
QUOTATION BOOK

Compiled by Andrew Russell

SOMERVILLE PRESS

Somerville Press Ltd,
Dromore, Bantry, Co. Cork, Ireland

©Andrew Russell 2017

First published 2017

Designed by Jane Stark
Typeset in Minion Pro
seamistgraphics@gmail.com

ISBN: 978-0-9955239-5-1

Printed and bound in Spain
by GraphyCems, Villatuerta, Navarra

Front cover photo:
William Butler Yeats photographed
by Alice Boughton in 1903

IT'S GREAT THAT PEOPLE
STILL CARE ABOUT BOOKS,
AND IT'S GREAT THAT
YOU CAN STILL FASHION
A LIFE FROM LITERATURE.

John Banville

WE THINK WE'RE LIVING
IN THE PRESENT, BUT WE'RE
REALLY LIVING IN THE PAST.

•

WRITERS ARE JUST LIKE
OTHER PEOPLE, EXCEPT
SLIGHTLY MORE OBSESSED.

John Banville

DOING WHAT YOU
DO WELL IS DEATH.
YOUR DUTY IS TO
KEEP TRYING TO DO THINGS
THAT YOU DON'T DO WELL,
IN THE HOPE OF LEARNING.

John Banville

WE WRITERS ARE SHY
NOCTURNAL CREATURES.
PUSH US INTO THE LIGHT
AND THE LIGHT BLINDS US.

John Banville

NOTHING MATTERS

BUT THE WRITING.

THERE HAS BEEN NOTHING

ELSE WORTHWHILE...

A STAIN UPON THE SILENCE.

Samuel Beckett

I HAVE MY FAULTS,
BUT CHANGING MY TUNE
IS NOT ONE OF THEM.

•

YOU'RE ON EARTH.
THERE'S NO CURE FOR THAT.

Samuel Beckett

James Joyce was
a synthesiser,
trying to bring in
as much as he could.
I am an analyser,
trying to leave out
as much as I can.

Samuel Beckett

WE ARE ALL
BORN MAD.
SOME REMAIN SO.

•

WORDS ARE
ALL WE HAVE.

Samuel Beckett

SAMUEL BECKETT IS A
GOOD FRIEND OF MINE.
I DON'T KNOW WHAT
HIS PLAYS ARE ABOUT,
BUT I ENJOY THEM.

Brendan Behan

CORKMEN AND NORTHERNERS

ARE THE HARDEST TO HANG...

THEY HAVE SUCH THICK NECKS.

•

HUNGER MAKES

PORNOGRAPHERS OF US ALL.

Brendan Behan

THE BIG DIFFERENCE
BETWEEN SEX FOR MONEY
AND SEX FOR FREE IS THAT
SEX FOR MONEY USUALLY
COSTS A LOT LESS.

Brendan Behan

YOU WOULDN'T
BE MINDING
THOSE POET FELLOWS.
THEY'RE A
DANGEROUS CLIQUE
AT THE BEST OF TIMES.

Brendan Behan

I HAD A VERY HAPPY
CHILDHOOD,
WHICH IS UNSUITABLE
IF YOU ARE GOING TO BE
AN IRISH WRITER.

Maeve Binchy

BECAUSE I SAW MY PARENTS
RELAXING IN ARMCHAIRS
AND READING AND LIKING IT,
I THOUGHT IT WAS A PEACEFUL
GROWN-UP THING TO DO
AND I STILL THINK THAT.

Maeve Binchy

I WAS VERY PLEASED OBVIOUSLY

TO HAVE OUTSOLD

GREAT WRITERS.

BUT I AM NOT INSANE...

I REALISE THAT I AM

A POPULAR WRITER WHO PEOPLE

BUY TO TAKE ON VACATION.

Maeve Binchy

I COULD WISH THAT THE
ENGLISH KEPT HISTORY
IN MIND MORE,
THAT THE IRISH KEPT IT
IN MIND LESS.

Elizabeth Bowen

IF YOU LOOK AT LIFE ONE WAY,
THERE IS ALWAYS
CAUSE FOR ALARM.

•

WHERE WOULD THE IRISH BE
WITHOUT SOMEONE
TO BE IRISH AT?

Elizabeth Bowen

CONTENTMENT

WAS MORE NOURISHING

THAN JOY.

BEING IN LOVE

WAS NOT VERY PEACEFUL.

Clare Boylan

THE PEOPLE OF THIS COUNTRY
ARE FULL OF KINDNESS,
BUT ALWAYS TO STRANGERS.
WHEN A RELATIONSHIP
IS REQUIRED – LANDLADY,
MOTHER, HUSBAND, WIFE,
COMPLICATIONS ARISE.
THEY DO NOT HAVE
A FACILITY FOR INTIMACY.

Clare Boylan

ALTHOUGH THE MAIDS
WERE THANKFUL FOR HOLY DAYS
AND WENT TO MASS, THEY WERE
REALLY MORE INTERESTED IN
AN OLD IRISH WORLD WHERE
FAIRIES, WITCHES AND BANSHEES
TOOK THE PLACE OF
OUR ANGELS AND SAINTS.

Mary Carbery

I'VE BEEN ASKED
WHY DOES IRELAND PRODUCE
SO MANY GREAT MUSICIANS,
AND THE ANSWER IS IT DOESN'T.
WHEN YOU COUNT THE
GREAT MUSICIANS IRELAND
HAS GIVEN THE WORLD
IN THE LAST TWENTY YEARS,
YOU CAN DO IT ON ONE HAND.

Roddy Doyle

ULYSSES COULD HAVE

DONE WITH A GOOD EDITOR.

YOU KNOW PEOPLE ARE ALWAYS

PUTTING *ULYSSES* IN THE

TOP TEN BOOKS EVER WRITTEN,

BUT I DOUBT THAT ANY OF THOSE

PEOPLE WERE REALLY MOVED BY IT.

Roddy Doyle

IT'S A BIG CON JOB.
WE HAVE SOLD THE MYTH OF
DUBLIN AS A SEXY PLACE
INCREDIBLY WELL;
BECAUSE IT IS A
DREARY LITTLE DUMP
MOST OF THE TIME.

Roddy Doyle

I HAVE A GREAT FANCY TO

SEE MY OWN FUNERAL

BEFORE I DIE.

•

SURELY IT IS MORE GENEROUS

TO FORGIVE AND REMEMBER

THAN TO FORGIVE AND FORGET.

Maria Edgeworth

PEOPLE SAY,
'AREN'T THE IRISH WONDERFUL.
SO MANY MARVELLOUS WRITERS.
SUCH A BEAUTIFUL PLACE.'
BLAH, BLAH, BLAH.
NO ONE BOTHERS TO TALK ABOUT
HOW POVERTY JUST WEARS YOU OUT.
HOW POVERTY IS A REALLY
STRESSFUL, SHAMING TRADITION.

Anne Enright

SOMETIMES BEING IRISH
FEELS LIKE A JOB YOU
NEVER APPLIED FOR.
I DON'T MIND BEING IRISH,
BUT I'M NOT A FAN
OF NATIONALISM.

Anne Enright

I LOVE EVERYTHING
THAT'S OLD –
OLD FRIENDS,
OLD TIMES,
OLD MANNERS,
OLD BOOKS,
OLD WINE.

Oliver Goldsmith

LIFE IS A JOURNEY
THAT MUST BE
TRAVELLED
NO MATTER HOW BAD
THE ROADS AND
ACCOMMODATIONS.

Oliver Goldsmith

SUCCESS CONSISTS OF
GETTING UP JUST ONE MORE
TIME THAN YOU FALL.

•

PITY AND FRIENDSHIP ARE
TWO PASSIONS INCOMPATIBLE
WITH EACH OTHER.

Oliver Goldsmith

ALL THAT A HUSBAND
OR WIFE REALLY WANTS
IS TO BE PITIED A LITTLE,
PRAISED A LITTLE
AND APPRECIATED
A LITTLE.

Oliver Goldsmith

I FEEL MORE AND MORE
THE TIME WASTED
THAT IS NOT
SPENT IN IRELAND.

Lady Gregory

IT'S A GOOD THING TO BE ABLE

TO TAKE YOUR MONEY IN YOUR HAND

AND TO THINK NO MORE OF IT

WHEN IT SLIPS AWAY FROM YOU

THAN YOU WOULD WITH A TROUT

THAT WOULD SLIP BACK

INTO THE STREAM.

Lady Gregory

I'VE ALWAYS ASSOCIATED THE
MOMENT OF WRITING WITH A
MOMENT OF LIFT, OF JOY,
OF UNEXPECTED REWARD.

•

A PERSON FROM NORTHERN IRELAND
IS NATURALLY CAUTIOUS.

Seamus Heaney

THE COMPLETE SOLITARY SELF:
THAT'S WHERE POETRY
COMES FROM,
AND IT GETS ISOLATED
BY CRISIS,
AND THOSE CRISES ARE
OFTEN VERY INTIMATE TOO.

Seamus Heaney

MISTAKES ARE THE
PORTALS OF DISCOVERY.

•

WHEN I DIE
DUBLIN WILL BE
WRITTEN IN MY HEART.

James Joyce

BETTER PASS BOLDLY

IN TO THAT OTHER WORLD,

IN THE FULL GLORY

OF SOME PASSION,

THAN FADE AND WITHER

DISMALLY WITH AGE.

James Joyce

THERE IS NO HERESY
OR NO PHILOSOPHY
WHICH IS SO
ABHORRENT
TO THE CHURCH
AS A HUMAN BEING.

James Joyce

...AND THEN I ASKED HIM WITH MY EYES
TO ASK AGAIN YES AND THEN HE ASKED ME
WOULD I YES TO SAY YES MY MOUNTAIN
FLOWER AND FIRST I PUT MY ARMS ABOUT
HIM YES AND DREW HIM DOWN TO ME SO HE
COULD FEEL MY BREASTS ALL PERFUME YES
AND HIS HEART WAS GOING LIKE MAD AND
YES I SAID YES I WILL YES.

(*Ulysses* Trieste-Zurich-Paris, 1914-1921)

James Joyce

IRELAND IS THE LAST BASTION OF CIVILISATION.

Molly Keane

A WRITER IS
NOT INTERESTED IN
EXPLAINING REALITY,
HE'S ONLY INTERESTED
IN CAPTURING IT.

Brendan Kennelly

I was drawn to feminism as a young woman because it was then called 'Women's Liberation'. It was about freedom. Today it is about equality. Freedom means differences always emerge; equality means freedom will be curtailed.

Mary Kenny

ONLY A BLOCKHEAD SAYS
'JE NE REGRETTE RIEN.'
REGRETS ARE PART OF THE
EXPERIENCE OF THOUGHT AND
REFLECTION, OF LEARNING
AND CORRECTING, OF DRAWING
LESSONS FROM FAILURE,
AND OF THE STRANGE, BITTERSWEET
SENTIMENT OF RUEFULNESS.

Mary Kenny

I'D RATHER DIG A DITCH
THAN GO TO A DINNER PARTY
WITH PEOPLE I DON'T KNOW.

•

MY TRUTH IS THAT WHAT DOESN'T
KILL YOU MAKES YOU WEAKER
RATHER THAN STRONGER,
ALTHOUGH IT MAKES YOU WISER.

Marian Keyes

I've always been
melancholic.
At a party, everyone
would be looking at the
glittering chandeliers
and I'd be looking at the
waitress's cracked shoes.

Marian Keyes

TAKE UP
CAR MAINTENANCE
AND FIND THAT THE CLASS
IS FULL OTHER THIRTY-
SOMETHING WOMEN
LOOKING FOR A FELLA.

Marian Keyes

GOSSIP IS MORE POPULAR
THAN LITERATURE.

•

I'VE ALWAYS ENJOYED
A WOMAN'S COMPANY
MORE THEN MEN'S.
THEY'RE USUALLY
BETTER LOOKING.

Hugh Leonard

THE PROBLEM WITH IRELAND IS THAT IT'S A COUNTRY FULL OF GENIUS, BUT ABSOLUTELY NO TALENT.

Hugh Leonard

IRELAND IS

A PECULIAR SOCIETY

IN THE SENSE THAT IT WAS A

NINETEENTH CENTURY SOCIETY

UP TO ABOUT 1970

AND THEN IT ALMOST BYPASSED

THE TWENTIETH CENTURY.

John McGahern

When I was in my 20s it did occur to me that there was something perverted about an attitude that thought that killing someone was a minor offence compared to kissing someone.

John McGahern

I THINK FICTION IS
A VERY SERIOUS THING,
THAT WHILE IT IS
FICTION, IT IS ALSO
A REVELATION
OF TRUTH, OR FACTS.

John McGahern

No, there's nothing
sweet in life as
love's young dream.

Thomas Moore

ROMANTIC LOVE IS AN ILLUSION.
MOST OF US DISCOVER THIS TRUTH
AT THE END OF A LOVE AFFAIR OR
ELSE WHEN THE SWEET EMOTIONS OF
LOVE LEAD US INTO MARRIAGE AND
THEN TURN DOWN THEIR FLAMES.

Thomas Moore

ONE OF THE SECRETS OF

A HAPPY LIFE IS

CONTINUOUS SMALL TREATS.

•

ONE DOESN'T HAVE TO GET

ANYWHERE IN A MARRIAGE.

IT'S NOT A PUBLIC CONVEYANCE

Iris Murdoch

I THINK BEING A WOMAN IS
A BIT LIKE BEING IRISH.
EVERYONE SAYS YOU'RE
IMPORTANT AND NICE,
BUT YOU TAKE SECOND BEST
ALL THE TIME.

Iris Murdoch

THE VOTE MEANS
NOTHING TO WOMEN.
WE SHOULD BE ARMED.

•

I'M AN IRISH CATHOLIC
AND I HAVE
A LONG ICEBERG OF GUILT.

Edna O'Brien

I HAVE SOME
WOMEN FRIENDS
BUT I PREFER MEN.
DON'T TRUST WOMEN.
THERE IS A BUILT-IN
COMPETITION
BETWEEN WOMEN.

Edna O'Brien

THE MAJORITY OF THE
MEMBERS OF THE IRISH PARLIAMENT
ARE PROFESSIONAL POLITICIANS,
IN THE SENSE THAT OTHERWISE
THEY WOULD NOT BE GIVEN JOBS
MINDING MICE AT CROSSROADS.

Flann O'Brien

EVERYWHERE I GO,
I'M ASKED IF I THINK
UNIVERSITY STIFLES
WRITERS. MY OPINION
IS THEY DON'T STIFLE
ENOUGH OF THEM.

Kate O'Brien

ALL THE WORLD'S A STAGE

AND MOST OF US ARE

DESPERATELY UNREHEARSED.

•

MONEY DOES NOT

MAKE YOU HAPPY,

BUT IT QUIETS THE NERVES.

Sean O'Casey

No man is as anti-feminist as a really feminist woman.

Frank O'Connor

PROGRESS IS IMPOSSIBLE
WITHOUT CHANGE,
AND THOSE WHO CANNOT
CHANGE THEIR MINDS,
CANNOT CHANGE
ANYTHING.

George Bernard Shaw

WE ARE MADE WISE
NOT BY THE
RECOLLECTION
OF OUR PAST,
BUT BY THE
RESPONSIBILITY
FOR OUR FUTURE.

George Bernard Shaw

IF YOU CANNOT GET RID OF THE
FAMILY SKELETON, YOU MIGHT
AS WELL MAKE IT DANCE.
JUST DO WHAT MUST BE DONE.
THIS MAY NOT BE HAPPINESS,
BUT IT IS GREATNESS.

George Bernard Shaw

A LIFE SPENT
MAKING MISTAKES
IS NOT ONLY
MORE HONOURABLE,
BUT MORE USEFUL
THAN A LIFE SPENT
DOING NOTHING.

George Bernard Shaw

BEWARE OF FALSE KNOWLEDGE;
IT IS MORE DANGEROUS
THAN IGNORANCE.

•

A GOVERNMENT THAT ROBS
PETER TO PAY PAUL,
CAN ALWAYS DEPEND
ON THE SUPPORT OF PAUL.

George Bernard Shaw

I LEARNED LONG AGO,
NEVER TO WRESTLE
WITH A PIG.
YOU GET DIRTY,
AND BESIDES,
THE PIG LIKES IT.

George Bernard Shaw

THERE ARE TWO
TRAGEDIES IN LIFE.
ONE IS TO LOSE
YOUR HEART'S DESIRE.
THE OTHER IS TO GAIN IT.

George Bernard Shaw

Won't you come
into my garden?
I would like
my roses to see you.

•

There's no possibility
of being witty without
a little ill-nature.

Richard Brinsley Sheridan

THE IRISH AND THE ENGLISH
UNDERSTAND EACH OTHER
LIKE THE FOX AND THE HOUND.
BUT WHICH IS WHICH?
AH WELL, IF WE KNEW THAT
WE'D KNOW EVERYTHING.

Edith Somerville and Martin Ross

VISION IS THE
ART OF SEEING WHAT IS
INVISIBLE TO OTHERS.

•

A WISE MAN SHOULD
HAVE MONEY IN HIS HEAD,
BUT NOT IN HIS HEART.

Jonathan Swift

MAY YOU LIVE ALL
THE DAYS OF YOUR LIFE.

•

BLESSED IS HE WHO
EXPECTS NOTHING,
FOR HE WILL NEVER
BE DISAPPOINTED.

Jonathan Swift

OF THE THINGS WHICH
NOURISH THE IMAGINATION,
HUMOUR IS ONE
OF THE MOST NEEDFUL.
AND IT IS DANGEROUS
TO LIMIT OR DESTROY IT.

John Millington Synge

WRITER'S BLOCK!
IT DOESN'T EXIST.
YOU LONG FOR
IDEAS TO GO AWAY
SO YOU CAN HAVE
AN IDEA OF PEACE.

Colm Tóibín

JOHN MCGAHERN
TAUGHT ME THAT
IT'S OK TO
WRITE REPEATEDLY
ABOUT THE SAME THINGS.

Colm Tóibín

SUFFERING IS TOO
STRONG A WORD, BUT
WRITING IS SERIOUS WORK.
I PULL THE STUFF UP
FROM ME – IT'S NOT
AS IF IT'S A PLEASURE.

Colm Tóibín

I VALUE MOTHERS AND

MOTHERHOOD ENORMOUSLY.

FOR EVERY INATTENTIVE OR

ABUSIVE MOTHER IN MY FICTION,

I THINK YOU'LL FIND A DOZEN

OR SO WHO ARE NEITHER.

William Trevor

There is an element of
autobiography in all fiction
in that pain or distress,
or pleasure, is based on the
author's own. But in my case
that is a far as it goes.

William Trevor

IF YOU STAY, EVEN IF YOU
GO TO PRISON, YOU WILL
ALWAYS BE MY SON...
BUT IF YOU GO, I WILL
NEVER SPEAK TO YOU AGAIN.

(Her views on Oscar Wilde fleeing
to France to avoid prosecution.)

Lady Jane Wilde

I CAN RESIST EVERYTHING

EXCEPT TEMPTATION.

•

IF YOU ARE NOT TOO LONG,

I WILL WAIT HERE FOR YOU

ALL MY LIFE.

Oscar Wilde

BETWEEN MEN AND
WOMEN THERE IS NO
FRIENDSHIP POSSIBLE.
THERE IS PASSION,
ENMITY, WORSHIP, LOVE,
BUT NO FRIENDSHIP.

Oscar Wilde

I AM SO CLEVER THAT
SOMETIMES I DON'T UNDERSTAND
A SINGLE WORD I AM SAYING.

•

I HAVE SIMPLE TASTES.
I AM ALWAYS SATISFIED
WITH THE BEST.

Oscar Wilde

IT IS ABSURD
TO DIVIDE PEOPLE
INTO GOOD OR BAD.
PEOPLE ARE EITHER
CHARMING OR TEDIOUS.

Oscar Wilde

ALWAYS FORGIVE YOUR
ENEMIES – NOTHING
ANNOYS THEM MORE.

•

THE WORLD IS A STAGE,
BUT THE PLAY
IS BADLY CAST.

Oscar Wilde

THERE ARE
NO STRANGERS HERE;
ONLY FRIENDS YOU
HAVEN'T YET MET.

William Butler Yeats

THE INNOCENT AND
THE BEAUTIFUL
HAVE NO ENEMY
BUT TIME.

•

WAS THERE EVER A DOG
THAT PRAISED HIS FLEAS?

William Butler Yeats

THE ONLY BUSINESS
OF THE HEAD
IS TO BOW A
CEASELESS OBEISANCE
TO THE HEART.

William Butler Yeats

LIFE IS A LONG PREPARATION FOR SOMETHING THAT NEVER HAPPENS.

William Butler Yeats

IRISH WRITERS' INDEX

John Banville (1945-), novelist 6

Samuel Beckett (1906-1989), novelist,
  dramatist and poet 10

Brendan Behan (1923-1964), playwright,
  wit and author 14

Maeve Binchy (1940-2012), short-story
  writer and novelist 18

Elizabeth Bowen (1899-1973), novelist
  and short-story writer 21

Clare Boylan (1948-), journalist and novelist . 23

Mary Carbery (1867-1949), author 25

Roddy Doyle (1958-), novelist, dramatist
  and biographer 26

Maria Edgeworth (1767-1849), novelist 29

Anne Enright (1962-), novelist 30

Oliver Goldsmith (1728-1774), man
of letters 32

Lady Gregory (1852-1932), dramatist. 36

Seamus Heaney (1939-2013), poet, essayist
and playwright. 38

James Joyce (1882-1941), novelist 40

Molly Keane (1904-1996), novelist and
playwright 44

Brendan Kennelly (1936-) poet, dramatist
and novelist 45

Mary Kenny (1944-) author, playwright
and journalist. 46

Marian Keyes (1963-), novelist and
non-fiction writer 48

Hugh Leonard (1926-2009), writer and
    dramatist............................51
John McGahern (1934-2006), novelist
    and short-story writer 53
Thomas Moore (1779-1852), poet........... 56
Edna O'Brien (1930-) novelist............. 58
Flann O'Brien (1911-1966), novelist and
    columnist.............................. 62
Kate O'Brien (1897-1974), novelist and
    dramatist 63
Sean O'Casey (1880-1964), playwright....... 64
Frank O'Connor (1903-1966), short-story
    writer and novelist...................... 65
George Bernard Shaw (1856-1950),
    playwright and man of letters............. 66
Richard Brinsley Sheridan (1751-1816),

dramatist and politician. 73

Edith Somerville (1858-1949) and Martin
   Ross (born Violet Florence Martin
   1862-1915), novelists 74

Jonathan Swift (1667-1745), man of letters . . . 75

John Millington Synge (1871-1909),
   playwright 77

Colm Tóibín (1955-), novelist . . . . 78.

William Trevor (1928-2016), short-story
   writer, novelist and playwright. 81

Lady Jane Wilde (1821-1896), poet and
   nationalist. 83

Oscar Wilde (1854-1900), aesthete, wit
   and dramatist. 84

William Butler Yeats (1865-1939), poet,
   playwright and founder of the Abbey Theatre 89